SAVING
Christmas

HOW GOD KEPT HIS PROMISE
THROUGH THE GENERATIONS

MIKE MINTER &
TRAVIS MᶜSHERLEY

Published by Reston Bible Church
45650 Oakbrook Court
Dulles, VA 20166
www.restonbible.org

First Printing: 2017

Printed in the United States of America

ISBN 978-0-9677188-0-4

Layout design: Jen Anderson

Editorial work: Jason VanDorsten and Mariel McSherley

Cover design: Travis McSherley

CONTENTS

Dedicated to the saints at
Reston Bible Church

INTRODUCTION

This book tells the story of the war on Christmas.

We know what you might be thinking: *Hasn't enough already been written about how everybody says "Happy Holidays" instead of "Merry Christmas" these days?*

It's true that we tend to use the phrase "war on Christmas" to refer to our cultural reluctance to attribute any spiritual significance to December 25. Though *that* may be an unfortunate trend, it is not what this book is about. And it is certainly not what the Bible is about. The real war on Christmas has much greater stakes—universal stakes, eternal stakes. It is a war that takes place on the grandest of scales between the kingdom of light and the kingdom of darkness. And it is a war that has already been fought—and won—by God Almighty Himself.

And where can you find the story of Christmas in the Bible?

To answer that question, your mind might go to Matthew 1 or Luke 2. "Today in the town of David a Savior has been born to you; he is the Messiah, the Lord" (Luke 2:11).

Maybe you would point to the prophecy of Isaiah 7:14: "The virgin will conceive and give birth to a son, and will call him Immanuel." Or Isaiah 9:6, which says that "to us a child is born, to us a son is given."

No doubt about it—those are wonderful and precious passages of Scripture on which to reflect when we think about the coming of the Lord. But what about Genesis 3? Joshua 2? Micah 5? The books of Ruth or Esther?

What if we told you that *the entire Old Testament* is telling the story of Christmas? That Christmas shows up on nearly every page? That each of the narratives is a link in a chain that reaches from Eden to Bethlehem? That the focus of Old Testament history was a war fought because somebody had to save Christmas?

This book provides an overview of that war, from beginning to glorious end, and the good, bad, and ugly people whom God used along the way. Over the span of thousands of years, God employed the most unlikely individuals and the most improbable circumstances to ensure that a baby would be born to a virgin in Bethlehem one holy night. He called murderers, liars, harlots, kings, queens, peasants, Jews, and Gentiles into His service— all sinners, you might notice. He made use of dreams, famines, plagues, and even governments. He used faithful people and faithless people. Because somebody had to save Christmas.

That's what we celebrate during this season—not just the birth of the Messiah, our Savior, "God with us," but also ultimate victory in the greatest war ever fought and the fulfillment of God's promise to redeem His people from the shackles of sin, death, and hell.

If you are a follower of Christ, we hope that this book will inspire you to worship the one and only King as you see how His sovereign hand has worked in every detail of every story to provide the way for salvation and eternal life. If you don't yet believe in Jesus, our prayer is that your spirit will be stirred as you learn about the incredible and dramatic events that led to Jesus' birth.

And may all of us be amazed by God's power and love as we consider the price that was paid to save Christmas.

— one —

DECLARATION OF WAR

*And I will put enmity between you and the woman,
and between your seed and her Seed; He shall bruise
your head, and you shall bruise His heel.*
Genesis 3:15 (NKJV)

The third chapter of Genesis opens in a world of complete peace. God has finished His creation and proclaimed it "very good." Earth's only two human inhabitants—Adam and Eve—enjoy perfect and unhindered relationship with each other and with their Creator. The couple has complete freedom to partake in anything their hearts desire, except for one tree that God has deemed off-limits, under penalty of death.

Then the enemy moves in. In the form of a serpent, Satan seeks to undermine God's authority, trustworthiness, and love by convincing Eve that an even better life awaits if she will just take a bite. Eve eats. Adam eats. In doing so, they have violated the holy standard and joined the side of the enemy. They are now at war against Almighty God.

In the immediate aftermath of their sin, Adam and Eve die spiritually, which means they experience separation from God. They also begin to die physically, their once immortal bodies now subject to decay.

The consequences go even further than that. The entire creation falls under the wrath of God's curse, mankind is banished from its garden paradise, and generation upon generation will now toil and struggle and suffer.

All seems to be lost forever, dark and hopeless. But then comes Genesis 3:15: "And I will put enmity between you and the woman, and between your seed and her Seed; He shall bruise your head, and you shall bruise His heel."

That verse is the pivotal point for humanity, and the cornerstone on which the whole Bible rests. God has declared war against Satan, and He has declared victory in that war! Genesis 3:15 also reveals how God will bring about His victory: through the "seed" (or offspring) of the woman. We must note here that the seed is *singular*. God is not sending a nation or a tribe to defeat the enemy, but a "He."

Something else peculiar about this pronouncement is that lineage is always traced through the *man*. Yet

God says that it will be the offspring of the *woman* who will crush the enemy's head. What is implied is that this promised Seed will have a unique birth, a miraculous birth, a virgin birth.

Satan will wound the Seed, but the Seed will crush him.

From here, the rest of the story will unfold. War has been declared. Christmas has been promised. Human beings have given themselves over to the kingdom of darkness, but their Creator will send a Rescuer to bring them back to the light. While man waits for his redemption to come, the enemy will be relentless in his efforts to thwart the rescue plan and prevent the Savior from arriving. But God will leverage the forces of good and evil throughout history to bring about the salvation of mankind.

Because somebody has to save Christmas.

THOUGHTS TO CONSIDER:

1. *Take a few minutes to read the rest of Genesis 3. Have you ever thought about this chapter being part of the Christmas story?*

2. *How did the serpent tempt Eve to eat the fruit? Why do you think she ate it? Why did Adam eat it?*

3. *What can you learn about God based on His responses to Adam and Eve's sin?*

— *two* —

TWO SONS, TWO SACRIFICES, TWO PATHS

*By faith Abel brought God a better offering than
Cain did. By faith he was commended as righteous,
when God spoke well of his offerings.And by faith
Abel still speaks, even though he is dead.*
Hebrews 11:4

Adam and Eve have introduced sin to the human race, and now their descendents will inherit a nature that is bent toward sin and hostile toward God. That is why Scripture says that "sin entered the world through one man, and death through sin, and in this way death came to all people, because all sinned" (Romans 5:12).

But even though the line of Adam will be saturated with enmity, hostility, envy, pride, and disobedience, God refuses to cut down that family tree. If He does, there will be no Christmas. The enemy knows this as well, and he sets out to corrupt and destroy the line that would bring the promised Seed.

This battle emerges right from the first generation, as Adam and Eve give birth to two sons: Cain and Abel. Cain will grow up to be a farmer, working the soil and harvesting fruit, and Abel will become a shepherd. Eventually, both men make offerings to the Lord, reflecting their respective career choices. Cain gives God some of his fruit harvest, while Abel sacrifices one of his best lambs. God is pleased with Abel's offering, but He rejects his older brother's.

Cain is beside himself with anger and jealousy, and he directs his rage toward his brother. He lures Abel into the field and kills him in cold blood. The first man ever born is the first murderer. However, Scripture reveals that Cain had an accomplice: "Do not be like Cain, *who belonged to the evil one* and murdered his brother. And why did he murder him? Because his own actions were evil and his brother's were righteous" (1 John 3:12, emphasis added).

What was so wrong with Cain's offering? It was a sacrifice without blood. That may seem like an odd distinction, but Scripture tells us why it matters. "In fact, the law requires that nearly everything be cleansed with blood, and without the shedding of blood there is no forgiveness" (Hebrews 9:22).

In essence, Cain was attempting to reconcile himself to God through his own efforts. Abel realized, on the other hand, that the seriousness of sin requires a sacrifice unto death.

How did Abel know that he needed to offer a blood sacrifice? He must have learned it from his parents, who learned it from God Himself. Before they were expelled from the Garden, Adam and Eve had become aware of—and ashamed of—their nakedness. So God used the skin of animals to cover their bodies and their shame. In doing so, He revealed that sin could not be paid for without loss of life.

Abel understood this and worshipped the Lord accordingly, which is why Scripture says that "by faith Abel brought God a better offering than Cain did. By faith he was commended as righteous, when God spoke well of his offering" (Hebrews 11:4).

Now Abel's own blood has been spilt, and his murderer is the only one left to carry the hope of the Lord's salvation to the next generation. But God is not going to use Cain in that role. Instead, He provides Adam and Eve another son, Seth—a name that means "appointed one." Because somebody has to save Christmas.

THOUGHTS TO CONSIDER:

1. *Do you see anything in this story that you have never thought about before?*

2. *How is God's sovereignty apparent in the lives of Adam and Eve's children?*

3. *What does sin and sacrifice have to do with Christmas?*

— *three* —

THE WORLD THAT THEN WAS

By faith Noah, when warned about things not yet
seen, in holy fear built an ark to save his family. By
his faith he condemned the world and became heir
of the righteousness that is in keeping with faith.
Hebrews 11:7

By the time Noah arrives on the scene, generations later, Satan seems to be on the verge of accomplishing his mission to corrupt the line of the Seed. Violence and immorality reign over the earth, and things are so bad that "every inclination of the thoughts of the human heart was only evil all the time" (Genesis 6:5). God's heart is grieved at the state of His creation, and there seems to be no other recourse than to wipe humanity from the earth and abandon the promise of Christmas.

Then come these precious words of hope: "But Noah found favor in the eyes of the Lord" (Genesis 6:8).

In a world thoroughly saturated with darkness, Noah is a lone beacon of light. Surrounded by all kinds of debauchery, he has stayed faithful to the Lord and obeyed His commands over hundreds of years. He stands as a "preacher of righteousness" (2 Peter 2:5), speaking truth to the deafest of ears and most hardened of hearts. So, in His mercy, God reveals to Noah that judgment is coming, but there is a way—only one way—to escape it.

God's means of judgment will be a flood that will bring destruction to every corner of the earth. His means of salvation will be a massive boat, an ark, that will transport those aboard from the "world that then was" (2 Peter 3:6 KJV) to the world that now is, the world in which you and I now live.

The Lord gives clear instruction to Noah regarding how to build the ark, down to the smallest detail. Scripture records many of those details, including the length and height and width of the ship, and even the dimensions of the window on top. However, that blueprint does not include the dimensions of the door. Why wouldn't the Bible reveal that information? It is to demonstrate that the door is wide enough to accommodate all who would believe!

And to point to the One who will someday be revealed as the door that all are invited to enter (John 10:9).

The apostle Peter later says that God "waited patiently" while the ark was being built (1 Peter 3:20), welcoming all to enter into its refuge. Anyone who walks through the door will be saved.

Nearly the whole world scorns God's wrath and rejects His provision of salvation. But Noah believes. Noah obeys. He builds the ark exactly as the Lord had instructed. When the floodwaters begin to rise, only Noah, his sons, and their wives are shielded from God's judgment.

Because of his faith, Noah has become an "heir of righteousness" (Hebrews 11:7). And because of his faith, we are all able to gain an immeasurable and eternal inheritance. The ark provided the only way for Noah's family to find physical salvation, and it will preserve, through the line of Noah, the only way for any of us to find spiritual salvation.

Because somebody has to save Christmas.

THOUGHTS TO CONSIDER:

1. Do you ever feel like the world is completely corrupt, the enemy is winning, or maybe God is not in control? How does your faith play into this?

2. How does Scripture give us glimpses into what is really going on, spiritually, behind the scenes?

3. Can you imagine being the only person on earth who is faithful to the Lord? What must that have been like for Noah and his family?

— *four* —

THE CALL AND THE COVENANT

The Lord had said to Abram, "Go from your country, your people and your father's household to the land I will show you. I will make you into a great nation, and I will bless you; I will make your name great, and you will be a blessing."
Genesis 12:1-2

Descended from Noah's son Shem, Abram is a childless 75-year-old man living in a pagan society with his 65-year-old wife, Sarai. Those are probably the last people you would expect to be a part of saving Christmas. Abram may not even know who the one true God is. But God knows Abram.

The first time the Lord ever speaks to Abram, He calls Abram to leave his home and family to go to a land he's never seen before. God says to "go," but He doesn't tell Abram where he's going.

In addition to the call, God makes a vow. He tells Abram that he will gain a great name and a great nation, that he will be exceedingly blessed, and that his lineage will bring blessing to "all peoples on earth" (Genesis 12:3). How can any of this be, when Abram and Sarai haven't been able to bear children?

Yet Abram obeys a God he doesn't know and follows Him to a place he hasn't heard of, to obtain a promise he never asked for and a son he can't conceive.

Years pass. A famine drives Abram and Sarai away from the land, and they retreat to Egypt. Even though Abram carries a promise from Almighty God, doubts set in. Abram fears that because his wife is so beautiful, the Egyptian leaders will have no qualms about killing him so they can take her. Abram tells Sarai to lie and say that she is his sister so that his life might be spared. Indeed, the Egyptians are so impressed by Sarai's beauty that they offer Abram the spoils of a king. God, however, brings the king himself only spoil—in the form of disease for the king and his household.

After this lapse of faith, the Lord does not retract His promise to Abraham. On the contrary, He reaffirms it in the most incredible way imaginable.

Though Abram laments that he still has no offspring—let alone a vast nation—God tells him that his descendants will be as innumerable as the stars above. Abram believes, "and it was credited to him as righteousness" (Genesis 15:6). Abram does not earn that righteousness, rather it is given to him because of his simple trust that God would do what He said He would do. Abram has faith that through his seed will come the ultimate Seed, by whom all nations will be blessed. This is a precedent that will follow God's people through the ages: Whenever someone places his trust in the Seed of the woman, the offspring of Abram, he will be granted the very righteousness of God Himself.

Abram still seeks some assurance. God has assured him that he will gain countless descendants and abundant land, but Abram boldly asks how he can be certain that God will come through. "Sovereign Lord," he says, "how can I know that I will gain possession of it?" (Genesis 15:8).

God responds by sealing His promise with a covenant. To make such a binding commitment today, we might call a lawyer and ask him to write up a contract to sign. If we later violated that deal, we might be required to forfeit finances, possessions, or personal freedom. In Abram's day, though, a covenant was a life-and-death matter.

God commands Abram to gather some animals, cut them in half, and position the halves across from each other. To complete the process, what normally happens is that both parties in the covenant walk through the blood of the slaughtered animals, graphically making the statement to each other, "May I be cut to pieces, like these animals, if I fail to keep this agreement."

The ceremony is prepared, but God knows that Abram could not possibly fulfill the obligations of this covenant. He would be doomed from the start, relying on his own efforts and strength. So the Lord places Abram in a deep sleep and, in the form of a "smoking firepot with a blazing torch" (Genesis 15:17), passes between the animals *by Himself.* This is no longer a two-party deal, but an unbreakable, unconditional covenant signed by the Creator of the universe. In effect, God is saying, "If I don't keep My part of this covenant, may *I* be cut to pieces."

Thus God, and God alone, will be the keeper of this deal. It provides a rock-solid assurance that God will hold secure those who belong to Him, knowing that we would fail every day to uphold our end of the bargain. Eventually, though, Someone *will* need to be cut in pieces to fulfill it.

For the covenant to be kept, the Seed must come to satisfy its conditions. And for the Seed to come, Abram's line must continue. Somebody still has to save Christmas.

THOUGHTS TO CONSIDER:

1. *What is the importance of God's covenant with Abram?*

2. *How does that covenant point to God's plan of salvation?*

3. *Can you ever fully keep your promises to God? How does God respond to that?*

— *five* —

ABRAHAM IS GIVEN THE SEED

*Now the Lord was gracious to Sarah as he had
said, and the Lord did for Sarah what he had
promised. Sarah became pregnant and bore
a son to Abraham in his old age, at the very
time God had promised him.*
Genesis 21:1-2

It has been years since God gave Abram the promise that
he would be the father of a great nation. But he and his wife
aren't getting any younger, so Sarai decides that it's time to
take matters into their own hands. She tells her husband
that since the Lord hasn't provided their family any
children, Abram should raise one through her handmaid,
Hagar. Abram agrees to this strategy and Hagar soon gives
birth to a son named Ishmael.

But this was not God's strategy. Abram has succeeded in
producing an offspring and a lineage, but he did it by his own

means and in his own way. The consequences of Abram's misguided action will be seen and felt for generations.

Thirteen more years go by. Abram is now ninty-nine years old, and Ishmael continues to be his only offspring. Still, God's plan has not been thwarted, and He reiterates to Abram that he and Sarai will indeed have a son together. It will be that son whom God will use to build the nation that He had promised Abram. And more importantly, it will be that son through whom God will bring Christmas.

To demonstrate that the covenant remains unbroken, God changes Abram's name. "No longer will you be called Abram; your name will be Abraham, for I have made you a father of many nations" (Genesis 17:5).

His wife's name is also changed. "As for Sarai your wife, you are no longer to call her Sarai; her name will be Sarah. I will bless her and will surely give you a son by her. I will bless her so that she will be the mother of nations; kings of peoples will come from her" (Genesis 17:15-16).

Abraham's response to this earth-shaking, heaven-sent pronouncement is...to laugh. A one-hundred-year-old man and a ninety-year-old woman will give birth to a son? That would be impossible, except God tells Abraham that it is exactly what is going to happen. Then He directs

Abraham to name the boy Isaac, which means "to laugh"—thus Isaac will be a living reminder that God is able to do the impossible to accomplish His purposes. And he will be a reminder that God's ways are greater than our ways.

Ishmael was born out of man's attempts to find his own salvation. Isaac will be born because God is faithful to His word. "For it is written that Abraham had two sons, one by the slave woman and the other by the free woman. His son by the slave woman was born according to the flesh, but his son by the free woman was born as the result of a divine promise" (Galatians 4:22-23).

Less than a year later, Sarah gives birth to Isaac. Because somebody has to save Christmas.

THOUGHTS TO CONSIDER:

1. *What promises from God in Scripture do you hold most dear? Why?*

2. *Has there ever been a time in your life where you took things into your own hands because you feared God wouldn't come through? What happened?*

3. *In which areas of your life do you need to grow in your trust of the Lord?*

six

ABRAHAM GIVES UP THE SEED

*"The fire and wood are here," Isaac said, "but
where is the lamb for the burnt offering?"
Abraham answered, "God himself will provide
the lamb for the burnt offering, my son." And
the two of them went on together.*
Genesis 22:7-8

God's vow to Abraham has finally been realized. Isaac
is here, Abraham's lineage is secure, and the plan of
redemption is on track. But then something surprising
happens. Something unthinkable. God tells Abraham to
take Isaac, his precious son, to the top of a mountain and
offer him up as a sacrifice. How can this be? God had
given Abraham a remarkable promise, and now, out of
His own mouth, He is commanding Abraham to kill the
promise. Is God Himself trying to derail Christmas from
coming? Of course not. It *is* going to be from the line

of Abraham, and the line of Isaac, that the Messiah will eventually come—somehow.

Even though the divine order is a heavy one, Abraham shows no signs of his past doubt. Scripture says that he arose "early in the morning" to begin the three-day journey to the mountain God had ordained (Genesis 22:3). He gathers wood for the offering, collects Isaac, instructs two servants to accompany him, and sets off to fulfill the solemn assignment.

When the party is within eyesight of the mountain, Abraham tells his servants to remain behind. "Stay here with the donkey while I and the boy go over there," he says. "We will worship and then we will come back to you" (Genesis 22:5). Wait just a minute—*we* will come back to you? How can Abraham say that, if he thinks his son is going to be offered up and slain?

It is because Abraham has learned to look *beyond* the promise; he has come to understand that the Lord can do far more than he could ask or think (Ephesians 3:20). Hebrews 11 reveals that Abraham is convinced that even the sacrifice of Isaac could not disrupt God's intentions or invalidate His covenant. He believes in the power of God over all of creation, and he "reasoned that God could even raise the dead" (Hebrews 11:19).

As father and son are walking alone together, Isaac seems to realize that something is amiss. "The fire and wood are here," he notes, "but where is the lamb for the burnt offering?" (Genesis 22:7).

Abraham's answer is a simple response of faith, but it is also a profound declaration of hope that will echo throughout the corridors of history: "God Himself will provide the lamb for the burnt offering, my son" (Genesis 22:8).

Abraham builds an altar in the spot God directs them to, and he puts Isaac on the altar and ties him down. He picks up a knife and is prepared to finish the mission, when he is suddenly stopped in his tracks by a voice from heaven. "Do not lay a hand on the boy," says the angel of the Lord. "Do not do anything to him. Now I know that you fear God, because you have not withheld from me your son, your only son" (Genesis 22:12).

Abraham has proven his faith. As he looks up, he sees that a ram has become caught in the thicket. He brings the ram to the altar and sets it in the place of sacrifice, while his son is set free. God has provided a substitute sacrifice and has spared Isaac, so that He might protect the line that will bring the ultimate Substitute, who will come to spare all who believe in Him.

Because somebody has to save Christmas.

THOUGHTS TO CONSIDER:

1. *In what ways does Isaac foreshadow the coming of Jesus?*

2. *In what ways does the ram foreshadow the sacrifice of Jesus?*

3. *How could Abraham be so confident that Isaac would return home with him?*

— *seven* —

TWO BROTHERS, ONE BLESSING

The Lord said to [Rebekah], "Two nations are in
your womb, and two peoples from within you will
be separated; one people will be stronger than the
other, and the older will serve the younger."
Genesis 25:23

Isaac grows up and Abraham wants to find a wife for his
son, with one stipulation—he does not want her to come
from the pagan peoples surrounding them. So he sends a
trusted servant on a journey to seek a bride from among
Abraham's relatives. God's hand guides the servant, as
recorded in Genesis 24, and leads him to a young woman
named Rebekah.

Isaac and Rebekah marry, but twenty years pass with
no children to carry the promised Seed. Isaac prays to the
Lord "on behalf of his wife" (Genesis 25:21), and God hears
his prayer and gives them twin boys.

While Rebekah is pregnant, God reveals to her that both of her sons will be patriarchs of mighty nations, but that, contrary to the customs of that day, the elder son will become a servant to the younger one. God's purposes are never bound by man's customs or reasoning. Thus it's the younger son who is destined to receive his father's blessing, and it's the younger son whom God has chosen to be the next step toward Christmas.

The boys arrive, and the firstborn is named Esau. His brother is named Jacob.

As they grow into men, Esau develops into a skilled hunter and outdoorsman. He is what we might call a "man's man." Jacob, on the other hand, prefers to stay close to home. Esau becomes the favored son of his father, and Jacob the favored son of his mother.

Time passes, and Isaac eventually knows that his life is drawing to a close. His eyesight has already begun to fail him. So he prepares to pass on the blessing, which he intends to give to his firstborn and favorite son, Esau. He pulls Esau aside one day and tells him to go out into the field and hunt some wild game for him. He tells his son, "Prepare me the kind of tasty food I like and bring it to me to eat, so that I may give you my blessing before I die" (Genesis 27:4).

Esau obeys his father and grabs his bow and arrows and heads out to comply with his father's wishes. But Rebekah overhears Isaac's instructions and decides to counter Isaac's plans so that her own favorite son, Jacob, can receive the blessing. She orders Jacob to go get two goats from the field, so that she can make Isaac a delicious meal. Then Isaac will give the blessing to Jacob before Esau returns.

Yet how will they convince Isaac that it is actually the older son who is bringing him the meal? "Jacob said to Rebekah his mother, 'But my brother Esau is a hairy man while I have smooth skin. What if my father touches me? I would appear to be tricking him and would bring down a curse on myself rather than a blessing'" (Genesis 27:11-12).

In order to make their deception credible, Rebekah gives Jacob some of Esau's clothes and covers his arms and neck with goat hair so that he will feel like Esau and smell like Esau.

The scheme is set and the meal is ready, so Jacob takes it to his father. Isaac is amazed that his son has returned from his task so soon, but Jacob credits his quickness to the Lord's favor. Also odd is that the man serving the meal has hair like Esau, but his voice sounds a lot like Jacob's. "Are you really my son Esau?" Isaac asks. "I am," comes the reply (Genesis 27:24). Isaac is dubious, but he ultimately trusts his hands and nose over his ears and eyes and grants the blessing to the son he believes to be his eldest.

Just as it had been told to Rebekah, her younger son has usurped the older in securing their father's blessing. What is tragic is that the blessing was *always* going to be Jacob's because God had ordained and guaranteed it. All of the scheming and manipulation was completely unnecessary—it would have been far better to have simply trusted the Lord and waited for Him to bring His will to pass. The consequences of this deception will be stark, affecting the rest of Jacob and Esau's lives, not to mention generations to come.

Yet God will honor the blessing given to Jacob, and He will keep His promise to bring the Messiah through Jacob's line. Because somebody has to save Christmas.

THOUGHTS TO CONSIDER:

1. *Do you ever find it difficult to trust the Lord? Why?*

2. *"God's purposes are never bound by man's customs or reasoning." How do you respond to this statement?*

3. *How might this story have gone differently if everyone involved had looked to the Lord for guidance rather than trying to manipulate the outcome?*

— eight —

TWO SISTERS, TWELVE SONS, ONE NATION

*Your descendants will be like the dust of the
earth, and you will spread out to the west and
to the east, to the north and to the south. All
peoples on earth will be blessed through you and
your offspring. I am with you and will watch
over you wherever you go, and I will bring you
back to this land. I will not leave you until I
have done what I have promised you.*
Genesis 28:14-15

Isaac had chosen Esau to be the son who would receive his
blessing and carry the promises of God to Abraham. God
chose Jacob. But because Jacob used deceptive means to
acquire that blessing, he now fears for his life. Trying to
manipulate God always has consequences, and deception
always creates obstacles.

Esau is devastated at the loss of the blessing he thought was his. And he is furious at the brother who took it from him. His heart is set toward murderous revenge. When Rebekah finds out about this plot, she tells Jacob that he needs to get out of town—quick. She instructs Jacob to go live with his uncle, Laban, for a short time, until Esau lets go of his anger. But this is the last time she will see her beloved son.

Jacob begins his journey and while camping for the night, he has a profound dream. In it, he sees a stairway with angels traveling up and down. Above the stairway, God is there, speaking to Jacob and powerfully confirming that the promises given to Abraham will be passed on through Jacob and his descendents. He vows, "All peoples on earth will be blessed through you and your offspring" (Genesis 28:14). Even though Jacob is on the run and fleeing the repercussions of his own actions, God is still with him and still protecting the promise of Christmas.

Jacob continues on and finally finds his uncle. He also meets Laban's two daughters, Leah and Rachel. Leah is the elder daughter, but Jacob finds himself captivated by the younger one. He is so smitten by Rachel, in fact, that he agrees to work for Laban for *seven years* in order to make her his bride.

Those seven years come and go, though to Jacob "they seemed like only a few days" because of his great love for Rachel (Genesis 29:20). The wedding ceremony is held, the guests eat and drink and are merry, and the marriage is consummated. But when Jacob wakes up the next morning beside his wife, "behold, it was Leah" (Genesis 29:25 NKJV)! The deceiver has been deceived.

Even though Jacob had chosen Rachel to be his bride, and thus a part of the line of the Messiah, God has again made a different choice. And just as He once took Jacob's deception and used it to bring His plans to pass, He is now using deception *against* Jacob to keep the promise of Christmas alive.

Jacob persists in his pursuit of Rachel, and he works for Laban another seven years to be able to wed her. So now Jacob is married to both sisters, but he gives all of his heart and love to Rachel, much to Leah's dismay. Leah yearns for her husband's love, and the Lord answers her cry with a blessing that she cannot possibly understand. "When the Lord saw that Leah was not loved, he enabled her to conceive, but Rachel remained childless" (Genesis 29:31).

Leah gives Jacob three sons—Reuben, Simeon, and Levi—and with each one, she desperately hopes that she will now gain her husband's affection. Then she has a fourth son, named Judah, and she says, "This time I will praise the Lord" (Genesis 29:35). And it's this son, whose name means "praise," whom the Lord has chosen to join the line of the expected Seed.

Another eight sons and a daughter will be born to Jacob through Leah, Rachel, and their two handmaidens, as the sisters continue to compete for Jacob's attention and love.

Jacob's family story is full of deception, manipulation, jealousy, envy, disobedience, and distrust of God. Yet God will utilize all of that to build a nation that He will call to Himself, and to preserve the line of the One who will come and forgive people of those very sins. Because somebody has to save Christmas.

THOUGHTS TO CONSIDER:

1. *What is revealed about God's character in the fact that He built His chosen nation upon such broken family dynamics?*

2. *Have you ever felt like your sin was too great for God to overcome? How does His Word address this?*

3. *What difficult situations in your life have you seen God redeem for a greater blessing or purpose?*

— *nine* —

JUDAH AND TAMAR

*You are a lion's cub, Judah; you return from
the prey, my son. Like a lion he crouches and
lies down, like a lioness—who dares to rouse
him? The scepter will not depart from Judah,
nor the ruler's staff from between his feet,
until he to whom it belongs shall come and
the obedience of the nations shall be his.*
Genesis 49:9-10

The biography of Judah, the son of Jacob who is divinely
selected to be the next ancestor of the promised Seed, may
be one of the most disturbing narratives in all of Scripture.
But it is also among the most powerful displays of how
God uses even the worst aspects of man to carry out His
good and sovereign will.

Following some family turmoil, which we will learn
about in the next chapter, Judah moves away from home
and chooses a bride from among the Canaanite people—

something his father and grandfather were explicitly warned not to do. Judah and his wife have three sons. The first one marries a young lady named Tamar, but due to the wicked life he is leading, he goes to the grave before they have any children. Judah then instructs his second son to marry Tamar and raise up offspring on his brother's behalf. But that son refuses and commits a grievous sin himself, and his life is also cut short without a descendent.

Judah sends Tamar back to her own father's house, with an implicit guarantee that she'll be able to marry Judah's third son when he comes of age.

The son grows up, but Judah has no intention of keeping his promise. As a result of this betrayal, Tamar may remain childless the rest of her life. And of even more significance—eternal significance—is that Judah's lineage may come to an end, and the hope of Christmas with it.

Tamar is desperate, and maybe even vengeful. So when she hears that Judah is taking a business trip, she decides to disguise herself as a prostitute and place herself directly along his path. The scheme goes as planned, as evil schemes often seem to do.

Judah has nothing to offer as payment for his immoral actions, but he gives the woman his staff and signet ring as collateral. When his servant later returns with a goat to pay the debt, Tamar is nowhere to be found. And the locals reveal that, actually, there haven't been any prostitutes around at all.

Three months later, word reaches Judah that Tamar is pregnant. He is furious and demands that his daughter-in-law be put to death for her infidelity. But Tamar is about to shed light on Judah's own dark deeds. "As she was being brought out, she sent a message to her father-in-law. 'I am pregnant by the man who owns these,' she said. And she added, 'See if you recognize whose seal and cord and staff these are'" (Genesis 38:25).

Judah is taken aback and realizes that his sins have caught up with him. "Judah recognized them and said, 'She is more righteous than I, since I wouldn't give her to my son Shelah'" (Genesis 38:26).

Tamar's life is spared and she gives birth to twin boys, one whose name is Perez. Though Perez comes from a union of deceit and disobedience, it is through his line that the Seed of the woman will come.

The depravity throughout this narrative is shocking, isn't it? Yet far more shocking is that God could—and would—choose to use this ugliest of situations as part of the fulfillment of His glorious promise. Because somebody has to save Christmas.

THOUGHTS TO CONSIDER:

1. *How do the evil actions of Judah and Tamar highlight the redemptive goodness of God?*

2. *How does the fact that God uses broken people and devastating situations to accomplish His good purposes encourage you?*

3. *What is something difficult or painful that you are asking God to redeem for good? What would it look like for you to trust Him in that?*

— *ten* —

THE DREAMER COMES

Then he had another dream, and he told it to his brothers. "Listen," he said, "I had another dream, and this time the sun and moon and eleven stars were bowing down to me."

Genesis 37:9

At this point, Jacob, of all people, should have realized that a parent's favoritism can be detrimental to a family. Yet sin tends to be generational, and Jacob follows in his father's footsteps. He makes no secret that his favorite wife is Rachel and his favorite son is Joseph.

Joseph is the eleventh son born to Jacob, but he is the firstborn of Rachel. Not only is Joseph near to his father's heart, but he is one of the most righteous figures in the Old Testament. Surely, this must be the son of Jacob who is destined to carry the promised Seed of Christmas, right?

In God's often mysterious sovereignty, Joseph is not the one. However, he is absolutely vital to the story. In fact, if any single facet of Joseph's life doesn't take place, then there can be no drama of redemption, and Christmas will not come.

When Joseph is seventeen years old, his father gives him a beautiful coat. As one might expect, this fans the flames of jealousy among Jacob's other sons. "When his brothers saw that their father loved him more than any of them, they hated him and could not speak a kind word to him" (Genesis 37:4).

To make matters worse, Joseph then tells his brothers about a pair of dreams he had, in which the family was depicted—in the form of wheat sheaves and stars—bowing down to him. Now the brothers are so filled with rage that they begin to plot Joseph's murder.

They see their opportunity when Jacob sends Joseph to check on the brothers while they are out with the flocks. "Look, this dreamer is coming!" they exclaimed when they saw Joseph in the distance. "Come therefore, let us now kill him and cast him into some pit; and we shall say, 'Some wild beast has devoured him.' We shall see what will become of his dreams!" (Genesis 37:19-20 NKJV).

Fortunately, Reuben, the oldest, jumps in to thwart this contemptible proposal. He suggests that they put Joseph in the pit, but they shouldn't kill him. Reuben intends to return later and set his brother free, but instead, Judah comes up with the idea to sell Joseph to a group of Ishmaelites who are passing by on their way to Egypt.

The brothers agree, and the dreamer is sold—but his story is just beginning.

What a beautiful, divine irony that the Ishmaelites, a people born out of Abraham's lapse in faith while waiting for God's promise, are now used by God to make sure that Genesis 3:15 will come to pass.

And what a beautiful, divine irony that in the brothers' effort to destroy Joseph's dream, their actions will end up fulfilling it. Because somebody has to save Christmas.

THOUGHTS TO CONSIDER:

1. *What were your family dynamics like growing up? How did that shape your faith, for better or for worse?*

2. *In what way does sin tend to be generational? How have you experienced or observed this?*

3. *Have you ever had a "lapse in faith"? What happened? Has it resolved?*

eleven

FROM A PIT TO A PRISON TO A PALACE

When his master saw that the Lord was with him and that the Lord gave him success in everything he did, Joseph found favor in his eyes and became his attendant. Potiphar put him in charge of his household, and he entrusted to his care everything he owned.
Genesis 39:3-4

Throughout Joseph's ordeal in Genesis 37, the name of the Lord is not mentioned. Strange, isn't it? Yet we find that in sections of Scripture where God's name is conspicuously absent, His providence is conspicuously present. And that presence will be profoundly revealed in the rest of Joseph's story.

Trapped in a pit and about to be killed by his own brothers, Joseph no doubt wondered whether he had been utterly abandoned. But he was not alone. God was with Joseph, sparing his life and bringing the Ishmaelite travelers by at just the right time. Now in Egypt, Joseph is sold yet again, this time to a government official named Potiphar. And Scripture says that "the Lord was with Joseph so that he prospered" (Genesis 39:2).

Potiphar is so impressed by Joseph's supernatural aid that he puts Joseph in charge of his entire estate. And the Lord's blessings to Joseph overflow onto Potiphar.

Unfortunately, Potiphar's wife is also quite impressed by Joseph, and she makes repeated attempts to express her romantic interest. Joseph refuses her advances, in deference to both his God and his Egyptian master, but she is undeterred. Eventually, Potiphar's wife turns the tables on Joseph and accuses him of trying to seduce her! Potiphar is angry, as could be expected, but apparently not angry enough to respond to this "crime" with capital punishment. Instead, he puts Joseph in prison—a strangely light sentence considering the weight of the accusations and considering Joseph's lowly status as a slave.

At this point, we may be tempted to pity Joseph. After all he's been through, and all he's done to remain upright and morally pure, how could he get such a raw deal? Yet

God knows exactly what He is doing, and He has still not abandoned His servant Joseph.

"But while Joseph was there in the prison, the Lord was with him; he showed him kindness and granted him favor in the eyes of the prison warden" (Genesis 39:20-21).

Once again, God pours blessing upon Joseph to the amazement of those around him. Once again, Joseph is elevated to a position of leadership and authority because of it. And once again, God has set him in exactly the right spot to protect the promise of Christmas.

Eventually, two new prisoners come under Joseph's care—the butler and the head baker of the Egyptian Pharaoh himself. One morning, both men seem especially downcast, and Joseph asks them a simple question that will change the course of history: "Why do you look so sad today?" (Genesis 40:6).

It turns out that both men are perplexed by dreams they'd had the night before. And it turns out that, with God's help, Joseph the Dreamer is able to interpret their dreams. So the men share what they saw, and Joseph gives one of them very good news and one of them very bad news. He tells the butler that he is about to be restored to his former employment, and he informs the baker that he will shortly be executed.

In three days, both interpretations prove true. Before the butler is released from the prison, Joseph makes of him a most reasonable request. "But when all goes well with you, remember me and show me kindness; mention me to Pharaoh and get me out of this prison. I was forcibly carried off from the land of the Hebrews, and even here I have done nothing to deserve being put in a dungeon" (Genesis 40:14-15).

The butler forgets Joseph, however, leaving him stuck behind bars—right where God needs him to be. The butler's slip in memory is providential because two years later, Pharaoh is troubled by his own strange dream. No one is able to tell the king what the dream means, and then the butler finally remembers a man in prison who might be able to help.

Joseph is brought to the palace. He reveals to Pharaoh that the dream is a warning. Egypt is about to experience seven years of abundance, but after that, seven years of famine will devastate the land. Joseph suggests that the nation can survive, however, if the workers of the land will set aside a portion of their harvest during the seven fruitful years. Then they can use that surplus to feed themselves during the drought—and they will be able to feed the surrounding nations as well.

Pharaoh is blown away by Joseph's insights. He asks his officials, "Can we find anyone like this man, one in whom is the spirit of God?" (Genesis 41:37).

And yet again, Joseph emerges from the depths of despair to rise to extraordinary influence, this time as second-in-command to one of the most powerful people in the world. Why? Because the Lord is with Joseph. And because somebody has to save Christmas.

THOUGHTS TO CONSIDER:

1. *Why is it important to remember that God is with us, even when we feel alone or abandoned?*

2. *How is God's sovereignty a comfort during trials or seasons of suffering?*

3. *What areas of influence has the Lord given you? Are you stewarding those well?*

— *twelve* —

WHAT GOD MEANT FOR GOOD

*But Joseph said to them, "Don't be afraid. Am I
in the place of God? You intended to harm me,
but God intended it for good to accomplish what
is now being done, the saving of many lives."*
Genesis 50:19-20

The famine comes, and Jacob's family realizes that they
cannot produce enough food to sustain their growing
numbers. But they have heard about the incredible
prosperity in Egypt, so in desperation, ten of Jacob's sons
journey south to buy provisions.

What they don't yet realize is that their fates will rest in
the hands of the one they had tossed into a pit and sold into
slavery some twenty years earlier. That means that Joseph
has had two decades for all of the abuse, hatred, jealousy,
betrayal, and injustice toward him to fester in his mind.
From a human standpoint, he would have every reason

to be embittered toward all of those who made his life so difficult—especially his brothers—and to use his position of authority to enact revenge at the first opportunity.

Such an opportunity comes when the brothers arrive in Egypt and end up face to face with Joseph. They don't recognize the boy, now grown up, whom they had sold to the Ishmaelites. But Joseph knows exactly who they are. He decides to keep his identity a secret for now, and he devises an elaborate test to find out whether they have repented of their evil deeds. He accuses the ten men of espionage and holds one of them, Simeon, hostage until the others can prove their innocence by returning with the younger brother, Benjamin, they claimed to have.

Jacob is devastated at the thought of sending his beloved youngest son Benjamin to face the dangers of a journey to Egypt. Yet eventually the food becomes scarce again, and he relents after Judah makes a solemn pledge to guard Benjamin's life. "I myself will guarantee his safety," Judah swears. "You can hold me personally responsible for him. If I do not bring him back to you and set him here before you, I will bear the blame before you all my life" (Genesis 43:9).

They arrive back in Egypt, and all eleven brothers end up bowing in Joseph's presence—bringing to pass the dream he dreamed so long ago. Joseph is overwhelmed with emotion at the sight of all of his brothers together, but he is not ready to reveal himself to them just yet.

In one final gauge of their integrity, Joseph hides a valuable silver cup in Benjamin's knapsack as the brothers pack up their rations and begin their trip back home. When the "theft" is discovered, Joseph declares that Benjamin must stay behind and remain his servant in Egypt. Thus the brothers find themselves in effectively the same scenario that had transpired those twenty years prior. Would they again abandon their little brother, sparing their own lives but destroying their father as he loses another adored son?

This time, Judah steps up and, instead of condemning his brother to a life of slavery, offers to take his place. He lays down his life, the innocent taking the punishment of the guilty. That action will cast a shadow across human history to point to One much greater than Judah—One who will come through his family line—who will lay down His life to pay the penalty for the sin of Jacob's sons and of all who would put their faith in Him.

Witnessing this noble sacrifice, Joseph can contain himself no more, and he reveals his true identity. The brothers are mortified. They brace themselves for the brunt of Joseph's wrath to fall on their heads. Instead, they receive unthinkable mercy and forgiveness. And Joseph demonstrates that he now understands God's sovereignty over the course of his life. "I am your brother Joseph, the one you sold into Egypt! And now, do not be distressed and do not be angry with yourselves for selling me here, because it was to save lives that God sent me ahead of you" (Genesis 45:4-5).

You sold me, but God sent me.

As powerful as Joseph has become, he takes a backseat and reminds his brothers (and you and me) that God is the hero of this story. He tells them, "you meant evil against me; but God meant it for good, in order to bring it about as it is this day, to save many people alive" (Genesis 50:20 NKJV).

Joseph knows that what his brothers did to him was profoundly wicked, but he also knows that God's plans cannot be thwarted. His story will be told. His promises will be kept. So Joseph offers his brothers grace, and leaves the righting of wrongs in the hands of the righteous Judge.

Jacob and his sons are thus spared from the effects of a great drought, and they are spared from the consequences of a great sin. As a result, the nation of Israel will take root and grow in the land of Egypt. Because somebody has to save Christmas.

THOUGHTS TO CONSIDER:

1. *How does a God-centered, eternal perspective help us deal with the difficult situations in life? Is there a situation you are dealing with to which you need to apply an eternal perspective?*

2. *Is there a relationship in your life that has caused bitterness in you? What would it look like for you to extend mercy, grace, and forgiveness to that person?*

3. *Is there an unreconciled wrong that you have done toward someone else that you need to trust God and take ownership of? What would it look like to trust God and take a step toward reconciliation with that person?*

— *thirteen* —

A DELIVERER DELIVERED

*By faith Moses' parents hid him for three
months after he was born, because they saw
he was no ordinary child, and they were not
afraid of the king's edict.*
Hebrews 11:23

Almost four hundred years have now passed since the family of Jacob packed up and moved to Egypt. In that time, the descendents of Jacob have multiplied to become twelve tribes and one nation, albeit a nation displaced from the land God promised Abraham they would inhabit. Still dwelling in Egypt, the people of Israel have so increased in number that the Egyptian leadership is getting nervous. And the rulers of Egypt have long since forgotten how God used Joseph to rescue their people from famine. "Then a new king, to whom Joseph meant nothing, came to power in Egypt. 'Look,' he said to his people, 'the Israelites have become far too numerous for us. Come, we must deal shrewdly with them or they will become even more numerous and, if war breaks out, will join our enemies, fight against us and leave the country'" (Exodus 1:8).

The new pharaoh's strategy will be an increasingly drastic and violent one. He first assigns taskmasters over the people of Israel, turning them into his slaves. Yet under this oppression, Israel continues to grow and flourish. "But the more they were oppressed, the more they multiplied and spread; so the Egyptians came to dread the Israelites and worked them ruthlessly" (Exodus 1:12-13). So the king increases the stakes even more by ordering the Hebrew midwives to kill every male child as soon as he is born. Not only is this a desperate attempt by Pharaoh to defend against the perceived threat of a Hebrew uprising, but it is also a desperate attempt by the evil one to break the line of the promised Seed.

Standing in Pharaoh's way—and Satan's—are two courageous midwives, Shiphrah and Puah. These ladies fear God more than they fear the king, and they make sure the Hebrew boys live. "So God was kind to the midwives and the people increased and became even more numerous" (Exodus 1:20).

With his efforts foiled again, Pharaoh takes things another step further and orders all of the Hebrew boys to be thrown into the Nile. But another brave woman named Jochebed valiantly undermines this sinister plot with a plan of her own.

When Jochebed's baby is born, she hides him for three months, but she realizes that her defiance will soon be discovered. So she decides that she will, in fact, put the little boy in the river—just not the way Pharaoh had intended. Jochebed lays the baby in a basket, or a little ark. (The Hebrew word is the same one used for the "ark" that preserved Noah and his family through the flood.)

Then she deposits the basket along the banks of the Nile, while her daughter Miriam watches "at a distance to see what would happen to him" (Exodus 2:4).

What happens is that the daughter of Pharaoh chooses to go down to bathe at that very spot. She notices the basket and asks for it to be brought to her. When she opens it and sees the baby crying inside, her heart is moved. She cannot bear the thought of the boy becoming a victim of her father's decree. Miriam seizes the moment and boldly asks, "Shall I go and get one of the Hebrew women to nurse the baby for you?" (Exodus 2:7).

Pharaoh's daughter thinks this is a great idea, so Miriam races off and brings *the baby's mother* to care for him. Jochebed is paid to nurse her own son—out of the pocketbook of the very government that was trying to kill him!

Eventually, Pharaoh's daughter adopts the baby and names him Moses.

The details of Moses' dramatic entry into the world are carefully outlined for us so that we don't miss the masterful hand of God at work. He brings about His will using everyday activities (like bathing), everyday items (like a basket), corrupt governments, and men and women who hold no earthly prestige but have immense heavenly prestige.

Like Joseph before him, Moses will spend much of his life in the palace of the Egyptian king. Whereas God used Joseph to save His people to bring them to Egypt, He will use Moses to save them by leading them out. Because somebody has to save Christmas.

THOUGHTS TO CONSIDER:

1. *Had you ever considered Moses' story as part of the Christmas narrative? How does this affect your view of Christmas?*

2. *Have you ever had to stand up for something you knew was right, even when others would not? What happened?*

3. *Where in your life do you see "the masterful hand of God at work"?*

— *fourteen* —

THE RELUCTANT LEADER

This is the same Moses they had rejected
with the words, "Who made you ruler and
judge?" He was sent to be their ruler and
deliverer by God himself, through the angel
who appeared to him in the bush.
Acts 7:35

Moses spends the first forty years of his life in Pharaoh's court, becoming educated in art, science, literature, and the Egyptian culture and language. Yet he never identifies himself as Egyptian. He is a citizen of Egypt by adoption, but he knows that he belongs to the people of Israel. The Book of Hebrews tells us that Moses "refused to be known as the son of Pharaoh's daughter. He chose to be mistreated along with the people of God rather than to enjoy the fleeting pleasures of sin" (Hebrews 11:24-25). Moses could have comfort, but he chooses affliction. He could have immense earthly wealth, but he pursues eternal treasures instead.

Consequently, when Moses sees an Egyptian beating one of his Hebrew kinsmen, he becomes enraged and kills the Egyptian. He thinks this deed was done in secret, but he finds out otherwise the next day, when he attempts to break up a fight between two Hebrew men. One of them says, "Who made you ruler and judge over us? Are you thinking of killing me as you killed the Egyptian?" (Exodus 1:14).

So now the Hebrews are angry at Moses, and the Egyptians want to avenge their fallen comrade. Moses sees no choice but to run away, and he flees to the desert of Midian, where he will spend the next forty years.

During that time, another brutal pharaoh comes into power in Egypt, and the people of God seek Him earnestly for rescue from their great oppression. God hears their cries and appoints Moses to be Israel's deliverer, and He conveys that message in a most unusual way—by speaking through a burning bush. He tells Moses to go back to Egypt, confront Pharaoh, and lead the people out of their servitude.

Moses is reluctant, to say the least. But he ultimately acquiesces and, along with his brother Aaron, approaches the king to ask him to let the Hebrew people go.

Pharaoh is reluctant, to say the least. So God sends a series of plagues that devastate Egypt's land, crops, livestock, and people. When the king continues to resist even after nine debilitating attacks, God prepares to send a tenth, which will take the life of every firstborn son in Egypt. The people of Israel will be spared this tragedy, however, if they place the blood of a lamb on their door post. God says, "The blood will be a sign for you on the houses where you are, and when I see the blood, I will pass over you" (Exodus 12:13). This won't be the last time in the course of history that God will use the blood of a Lamb to save many from the clutches of death.

The weight of this loss of life is too much to bear, and the people of Egypt urge the people of Israel to get out, as quickly as possible. Moses gathers the vast group together and leads them away as they start the journey toward their promised land.

It isn't long, though, before Pharaoh realizes that he has made a grave mistake in allowing his labor force to depart.

He gathers his army and his chariots and sends them in furious pursuit of the Israelites.

Shockingly, God guides His people to a spot where they are trapped between the mountains and the Red Sea, with no way to escape the pending onslaught. It is a hopeless situation and the Israelites are terrified. Yet Moses has come to understand that the promises of Almighty God will be fulfilled, no matter how bleak the circumstances. With great faith, he proclaims to the people, "Do not be afraid. Stand firm and you will see the deliverance the Lord will bring you today. The Egyptians you see today you will never see again. The Lord will fight for you; you need only to be still" (Exodus 14:13-14).

The Lord does indeed fight for His people, and He displays His power with the greatest miracle recorded in the Old Testament. As Moses stretches his hand over the Red Sea, God rips the waters from their course and holds them back so that His nation can walk through a path of dry land. Israel crosses to the other side, and as the Egyptians are giving chase, the Lord releases His grip and brings the sea crashing down upon them. "And when the Israelites saw the mighty hand of the Lord displayed against the Egyptians, the people feared the Lord and put their trust in him and in Moses his servant" (Exodus 14:31).

God had brought His people to an impossible predicament, so that He alone would get the glory when He brought them out. Because somebody has to save Christmas.

THOUGHTS TO CONSIDER:

1. *Why do you think Moses would choose affliction over comfort?*

2. *Have you ever been in an impossible predicament, where you felt trapped? What happened?*

3. *Is there a current situation in which you need to trust that "the Lord will fight for you; you need only to be still"?*

— fifteen —

WANDERING IN THE WILDERNESS

*But it was because the Lord loved you and
kept the oath he swore to your ancestors that
he brought you out with a mighty hand and
redeemed you from the land of slavery, from
the power of Pharaoh king of Egypt. Know
therefore that the Lord your God is God; he is
the faithful God, keeping his covenant of love
to a thousand generations of those who love
him and keep his commandments.*
Deuteronomy 7:8-9

The Israelites have escaped the heavy hand of their oppressors, but now they are a people without a land. Actually, they do have a land—the land that was promised to Abraham more than four hundred years earlier. God is prepared to fulfill that promise and bring His people to the home that has been awaiting them for centuries, but the journey to get there will end up taking another four decades.

During that time, God will preserve and protect the nation of Israel and the line of the promised Seed, all the while reminding them of His greatness and goodness.

When the people are hungry with no way to acquire sustenance, the Lord provides a supernatural bread that literally drops from the sky every morning (Exodus 16). This "manna" points to the Bread of Life who will one day come so that those who eat of it can live forever (John 6:35).

When the people are thirsty, with no source of water to be found, God brings forth water from a rock (Exodus 17:1-7). That rock foreshadows the eternal Rock from whom will flow living water (1 Corinthians 10:4).

Because God wants to set apart His people from the nations around them, He gives them laws to follow that guide how to worship, how to act, and how to live. This law anticipates the One who will eventually come to fulfill it (Matthew 5:17-18).

Because the Lord wants to be close to His people, He gives them instructions for building a tabernacle, a portable structure where the glory of God can dwell among them.

The tabernacle points toward the day when the Word will become flesh and dwell among us (John 1:14).

Because sin needs to be dealt with, God shows Israel how to make offerings and animal sacrifices that will provide atonement, or a covering, for their sin. Ultimately, though, they will need the Lamb of God to come and take away the sin of the world (John 1:29).

Despite all of the ways God has demonstrated His faithfulness to Israel, the people fear. They complain. They grumble. They doubt. They even craft idols to worship instead of their Lord. And because of their lack of faith in God's protection, He condemns an entire generation to wander around the wilderness instead of entering the land. It will be their children who get to march into that precious territory.

On multiple occasions, God seems ready to wipe out His unfaithful nation, but Moses intervenes on their behalf and pleads for mercy. "Turn from your fierce anger; relent and do not bring disaster on your people. Remember your servants Abraham, Isaac and Israel, to whom you swore by your own self: 'I will make your descendants as numerous as the stars in the sky and I will give your descendants all this land I promised them, and it will be their inheritance forever'" (Exodus 32:12-13).

Moses begs God not to forget all that He has promised. Because somebody has to save Christmas.

THOUGHTS TO CONSIDER:

1. *Have you ever been through a spiritual "wilderness experience"? What happened?*

2. *In what ways have you seen God provide for you? How have you experienced His faithfulness?*

3. *What reminders of God's greatness and goodness has He given you?*

— *sixteen* —

AN UNLIKELY RESCUER

*But Joshua spared Rahab the prostitute, with her
family and all who belonged to her, because she
hid the men Joshua had sent as spies to Jericho—
and she lives among the Israelites to this day.*
Joshua 6:25

Moses has died, the forty-year detour in the desert has
come to an end, and the time has arrived for Israel to enter
the land. God has chosen Joshua to be Moses' successor
and lead the people into their new home—and into battle.

Joshua sends two spies to a city called Jericho to assess
the situation there. They take quarters in the residence of
a woman named Rahab, who is a prostitute. Word gets
around that Israel has spies lurking in town, and the king
sends soldiers to Rahab's house to find them.

Fortunately, Rahab has heard stories about the God
of Israel, and she believes them. She fears God, and she

knows that her city stands no chance against an army whose Commander is the Lord. "I know that the Lord has given you this land and that a great fear of you has fallen on us, so that all who live in this country are melting in fear because of you" (Joshua 2:9).

So she hides the spies and tells the soldiers that she did meet them, but she has no idea where they went. When the coast is clear, Rahab pleads with the spies to provide protection for her family when they return to attack the city. They swear to keep Rahab's family safe as long as she continues to hide their identity from city officials. She agrees.

The spies keep their word and when the invasion finally begins, Joshua commands his army to make sure that Rahab and her family emerge unharmed. The spies bring them out of the city so that they can live peacefully among the people of Israel. It's a good thing they do, because Rahab's role in the story goes far beyond anything Joshua or his soldiers could have imagined.

It has already been an incredible story. After all, God has reached down into an enemy city, which He had doomed for destruction, and pulled out—of all people—a prostitute to rescue two of Israel's bravest troops. But He actually intends to make her a part of rescuing many, many more people than that.

As Rahab settles into her new life in a new nation, she marries a man out of the tribe of Judah. God chooses this marriage, and this couple, to carry the sacred lineage of the promised Seed. Because somebody has to save Christmas.

THOUGHTS TO CONSIDER:

1. *Rahab feared God and acted accordingly. What does it mean to fear God?*

2. *Why do you think that God consistently uses such unlikely people to enact His plans?*

3. *Think back over the chapters of this book you've read so far. How has your perspective on Christmas changed up to this point?*

— *seventeen* —

RUTH AND THE KINSMAN REDEEMER

But Ruth replied, "Don't urge me to leave you or
to turn back from you. Where you go I will go,
and where you stay I will stay. Your people will
be my people and your God my God."
Ruth 1:16

God has made His people victorious in battle, and He has finally brought them back into the land that their forefathers left centuries ago. But the war for Christmas is far from over.

Despite the Lord's faithfulness in giving to Israel all that He said He would, the people continue to rebel against Him, ignore the law given to Moses, and follow after other gods. In response, God withholds His mighty hand of protection from Israel, allowing their enemies to conquer and humble them. When the people finally cry out to God for help, He enlists liberators, in the form of judges, to restore peace and freedom. But this cycle of sin, discipline, and deliverance keeps repeating itself. "Whenever the Lord raised up a judge for them, he was with the judge and saved them out of the hands of their enemies as long as the judge lived; for the Lord relented because of their groaning under those who oppressed and afflicted them. But when the judge died, the people returned to ways even more corrupt than those of their ancestors, following other gods and serving and worshiping them. They refused to give up their evil practices and stubborn ways" (Judges 2:18-19).

In the midst of this tumultuous time, God once again weaves difficult circumstances and simple people to ensure that His promises are fulfilled.

A famine has come to the land, and a man named Elimelech decides to flee from his hometown of Bethlehem to the country of Moab, along with his wife Naomi and their two sons. In this foreign country, each son finds a wife, one named Orpah and one named Ruth.

Tragically, during the next several years Elimelech and both of his sons die, leaving behind three distraught widows. Orpah and Ruth are determined to remain with their mother-in-law, but Naomi pleads with the women to go back to their parents and start their lives over with new husbands. Orpah eventually complies and goes back home. But Ruth pledges to stick with Naomi the rest of her life, even though it will mean moving to Israel and living as an outsider and probably an outcast. In a profound expression of devotion, she begs Naomi, "Don't urge me to leave you or to turn back from you. Where you go I will go, and where you stay I will stay. Your people will be my people and your God my God" (Ruth 1:16).

Naomi and Ruth travel back to Bethlehem. They don't have any money or food, but the barley harvest is coming in, so Ruth offers to go work in the fields and gather excess grain.

Ruth's dedication and hard work do not go unnoticed, especially by the owner of the field, who just so happens to be a man named Boaz. Boaz just so happens to be the son of Rahab, the harlot from Jericho who rescued the Israelite spies. And he just so happens to be a close relative of Naomi's late husband. He is not merely related; he is also a *kinsman redeemer*, which means that, according to the law, he is eligible to recover Elimelech's land and to provide an heir for the family by marrying Ruth.

When Ruth comes home that night with so much food that she can barely carry it, Naomi knows that someone is showing her daughter-in-law special attention. Ruth tells her that the gracious landlord is Boaz, and Naomi's heart fills with hope. "The Lord bless him!" she exclaims. "He has not stopped showing his kindness to the living and the dead" (Ruth 2:20).

Not wasting any time, Naomi instructs Ruth to visit Boaz secretly at the threshing floor where he is working, and to place herself at his feet when he lies down to rest. Such a maneuver might seem peculiar to us, or maybe even scandalous, but Ruth is actually asking Boaz, in a beautifully humble way, for his protection and care. It is, in effect, a marriage proposal.

Boaz is greatly moved by the request. He is more than happy to perform his duties as the kinsman redeemer, but he reveals that there is another man who is an even closer relative and would therefore be owed the first opportunity. Fortunately, that man is either unable or unwilling to marry Ruth.

So Boaz buys back the land that had belonged to Elimelech, he takes Ruth as his bride, and together they have a son named Obed. Later, Obed will have a son named Jesse. And Jesse will have a son named David. And through the line of David will come the One who will be the ultimate Kinsman Redeemer.

In Ruth and Naomi's lives, exceptional tragedy has transformed into exceptional faithfulness, exceptional kindness, and exceptional sacrifice. And God will use it to bring about His exceptional promise. Because somebody has to save Christmas.

THOUGHTS TO CONSIDER:

1. *What characteristics of Ruth and Naomi stand out to you? What do you learn from their accounts?*

2. *Consider how Boaz's acts of kindness and sacrifice not only shaped the course of his own life, but played into God's great redemptive plan. Where do you need to exercise kindness and sacrifice?*

3. *How do you think Boaz points us to the ultimate Kinsman Redeemer?*

— *eighteen* —

THE ROYAL LINE EMERGES

After removing Saul, he made David their king.
God testified concerning him: "I have found
David son of Jesse, a man after my own heart;
he will do everything I want him to do."
Acts 13:22

Israel pleads with God to give them a king. Even though their request is made out of a lack of faith, and ultimately a rejection of God's kingship (1 Samuel 8:7), the Lord gives the people their king: a man from the tribe of Benjamin named Saul. He takes the throne, but it isn't long before he disobeys the commands of God and disqualifies himself from leadership.

God sends His prophet Samuel to anoint Saul's successor from among the sons of Jesse, the grandson of Boaz and Ruth. Jesse introduces his oldest son—a tall, strapping boy—and Samuel is sure he's found the future king. But God tells him otherwise: "Do not consider his appearance or his height, for I have rejected him. The Lord does not look at the things people look at. People look at the outward appearance, but the Lord looks at the heart" (1 Samuel 16:7). Jesse calls forward all of his other sons, except for the youngest who is still out caring for the sheep. But it is that young boy, David, whom God has actually chosen to lead His people—and to carry the line of the promised Seed.

As David begins to rise in fame and military prowess, Saul does not take it well. He becomes consumed by jealousy toward his divinely appointed replacement. He spends years plotting against David, hunting him down, and, on more than one occasion, trying to impale him with a javelin. But God protects David and His promise. David, for his part, has several opportunities to take vengeance— and the throne—by force, but he refuses to do so out of fear of the Lord.

When Saul eventually takes his own life on the battlefield (1 Samuel 31:4), David responds with grief, not joy. He soberly emerges from hiding and takes his place as king over Israel. As king, David grows in strength and leads Israel to numerous military victories. "And he became more and more powerful, because the Lord God Almighty was with him" (2 Samuel 5:10).

But on one spring day, David stays home from fighting and takes a walk along the palace roof. He spots a beautiful young woman, Bathsheba, taking a bath below him. Lust takes over and he orders the woman to be brought to him so that he can sleep with her. As if that is not bad enough, when Bathsheba discovers that she is pregnant, David schemes to have her husband Uriah, a faithful member of the king's army, killed in battle.

The consequences of these sins will be severe for David personally and the nation of Israel collectively. The baby born to David and Bathsheba will die as an infant, and David will never see the end of war. God rebukes him through the prophet Nathan: "Now, therefore, the sword will never depart from your house, because you despised me and took the wife of Uriah the Hittite to be your own" (2 Samuel 12:10).

David is crushed with guilt and repents of his wickedness. He confesses to the Lord, "Against you, you only, have I sinned and done what is evil in your sight; so you are right in your verdict and justified when you judge" (Psalm 51:4).

God shows mercy—incredible, redemptive mercy. David and Bathsheba have another child, a son they name Solomon. Out of David's many sons, Solomon is the one whom God chooses to inherit the throne of Israel and, more importantly, to continue the line of the promised Seed.

God will keep the covenant that He made with David early in his reign. "Your house and your kingdom will endure forever before me; your throne will be established forever" (2 Samuel 7:16).

Because somebody has to save Christmas.

THOUGHTS TO CONSIDER:

1. *Why does David say he sinned against God and God only (Psalm 51:4)?*

2. *How does the account of David, Uriah, and Bathsheba show God's unrelenting goodness yet again?*

3. *What warnings or encouragements do you take from this narrative?*

— *nineteen* —

KINGS AND PROPHETS

*Now, Lord, the God of Israel, keep for your
servant David my father the promises you
made to him when you said, "You shall never
fail to have a successor to sit before me on
the throne of Israel, if only your descendants
are careful in all they do to walk before me
according to my law, as you have done."*
2 Chronicles 6:16

God has now made clear that the promised Seed will come through the royal line of King David. And the evil one will make clear that he intends to disrupt the Lord's plan by corrupting or destroying David's descendants, along with the people of Israel. And he doesn't waste any time.

King Solomon, the son of David and Bathsheba, takes over the throne from his father and God blesses him with more wisdom, more power, and more wealth than anyone else in the entire world. But then he accumulates wives—literally hundreds of them—who turn his heart away from the Lord. He begins to follow their gods and set up shrines to them. In response to this, God declares that the kingdom will be ripped away from Solomon's son and given to someone outside of the royal line. But it can't be completely ripped away, since Christmas still has to come. So God says, "Yet I will not tear the whole kingdom from him, but will give him one tribe for the sake of David my servant and for the sake of Jerusalem, which I have chosen" (1 Kings 11:13).

That is exactly what happens. During the reign of Solomon's son Rehoboam, the kingdom splits in two. The northern tribes carry the name of Israel, and they are led by a series of wicked men who plunge the nation into moral depravity and spiritual devastation. They will ultimately be obliterated by the Assyrians and essentially wiped off the map.

Thus the hope of the eternal kingdom is contained in the southern tribes, collectively called Judah. The kings of Judah are not generally as evil as their northern counterparts, but they are far from perfect. God sets King David as the benchmark against which He judges the kings' righteousness, and most fall well short of that standard.

Some of them start out well, faithfully following the Lord, but then they are lured away by immorality, power, fear, or pride. Of King Uzziah, Scripture says that "after Uzziah became powerful, his pride led to his downfall" (2 Chronicles 26:16).

Some, like King Asa, make alliances with other kings and nations instead of trusting the Lord for His guidance and protection (2 Chronicles 16:7-9). Some are thoroughly wicked and lead the people to pursue false gods. King Ahaz is among the most depraved, even sacrificing his son to the Assyrian deities he worshipped. But those gods "were his downfall and the downfall of all Israel" (2 Chronicles 28:23).

Some are the victims of assassination, by perpetrators both foreign and domestic. Some take the throne by force, and others have it taken from them by force. When Jehoram becomes king, one of his first acts is to have all of his brothers executed. Then his violent rule comes to an end when his own family is killed or captured, and Jehoram is struck with a horrible disease. Scripture records this sobering epitaph: "He passed away, to no one's regret, and was buried in the City of David, but not in the tombs of the kings" (2 Chronicles 21:20).

Violence follows his only remaining son, Ahaziah, a wicked Judean king who is executed by the king of northern Israel. Then Ahaziah's mother, Athaliah, attempts to wipe out the entire royal line by murdering all of his sons. She nearly succeeds, except Ahaziah's sister manages to take one of the sons into hiding—a baby named Joash.

Athaliah sets herself up as queen and rules Judah for six years, until Joash is installed as king in a dramatic, covert operation (2 Chronicles 23). In his early years as king, Joash follows the Lord faithfully and restores much of the damage that his parents and grandparents had done to the temple. Later on, however, he follows their corrupt example and gives his heart to other gods.

Still, there are a few bright spots. King Hezekiah serves God faithfully, and he leads efforts to purify the temple and restore sacrifices and worship. So when the king of Assyria sends thousands upon thousands of soldiers to invade Jerusalem, God hears the prayers of Hezekiah. He supernaturally intervenes and destroys the invading army.

A couple generations later, King Josiah rediscovers the Word of God and strives to remove all traces of the apostasy that has tarnished the nation. "Neither before nor after Josiah was there a king like him who turned to the Lord as he did—with all his heart and with all his soul and with all his strength, in accordance with all the Law of Moses" (2 Kings 23:25).

Lamentably, the faithfulness of Hezekiah and Josiah is not enough to stave off the faithlessness of Judah. There are more wicked kings than righteous ones. And even when God sends His prophets, like Elijah or Isaiah or Jeremiah, to rebuke a king or remind him of the Lord's commands, their words are typically ignored—or they are tossed in prison.

Yet in spite of the immorality, the violence, the disobedience, and the idolatry of the royal family, God will make sure that the line of David continues. Because somebody has to save Christmas.

THOUGHTS TO CONSIDER:

1. *Notice that the pattern in David's life was the same as many of the kings who followed him—they started off diligently following the Lord, but were later lured away. What lured them away? What lures you away from the Lord?*

2. *What warnings are here for us when we are tempted to trust primarily in earthly rulers?*

3. *Where do you see the issue of worship interwoven in these narratives? Why is this important?*

— *twenty* —

HOPE AMIDST EXILE

*This is what the Lord Almighty says: "The people
of Israel are oppressed, and the people of Judah as
well. All their captors hold them fast, refusing to
let them go. Yet their Redeemer is strong; the Lord
Almighty is his name. He will vigorously defend
their cause so that he may bring rest to their land,
but unrest to those who live in Babylon."*
Jeremiah 50:33-34

God has spent generation after generation warning His
people that there will be consequences if they don't remain
faithful to Him. The northern kingdom of Israel has
already been carried off into exile, and if Judah doesn't
heed Israel's example, they are destined for a similar fate.
Through the prophet Jeremiah, God tells Judah, "This is
what the Lord Almighty, the God of Israel, says: Reform
your ways and your actions, and I will let you live in this
place" (Jeremiah 7:3).

They refuse to listen, and God's justice finally comes due. He carries out their punishment through the mighty Babylonian army, which ransacks Judah and takes captive its brightest and best citizens. Yet even though the nation has lost its way, God will not cease to preserve His people, along with the line of the promised King.

Among those who are brought to Babylon are four extraordinary servants of the Lord: Daniel, Hananiah, Mishael, and Azariah. (The latter three are often referred to by their more familiar Babylonian names: Shadrach, Meshach, and Abednego.)

Like Joseph before them, each of these men stays true to the Lord and worships Him, even while living in a foreign country, and no matter the cost. When their obedience to the law of God inevitably conflicts with the law of the land, Hananiah, Mishael, and Azariah are sentenced to death by fiery furnace (Daniel 3), and Daniel is condemned to a den of lions (Daniel 6). Despite the threat of execution, their faithfulness doesn't waver, and God miraculously delivers them, to the amazement of the kings.

Like Joseph, the men's piety leads them to be selected as royal advisers. Like Joseph, Daniel will be given the supernatural ability to interpret the dreams of a king. Like

Joseph, Daniel so impresses the king by the interpretation that he will be elevated to a position of unmatched authority. And once again, God uses that position to navigate His people through dark times.

Daniel watches kingdoms rise and fall. He sees the Babylonians displaced by the Medes, and the Medes supplanted by the Persians. With each new regime, he retains his royal influence, and he holds on to his confidence that the Lord has not forgotten His people. And even though he is, by all accounts, a righteous man, Daniel confesses on behalf of Judah and Israel: "We and our kings, our princes and our ancestors are covered with shame, Lord, because we have sinned against you" (Daniel 9:8).

Then he humbly pleads for God to restore His people and their nation. "Give ear, our God, and hear; open your eyes and see the desolation of the city that bears your Name. We do not make requests of you because we are righteous, but because of your great mercy" (Daniel 9:18).

The Lord hears Daniel's prayer, and He will bring His people out of exile and back into their land, because He is forgiving and faithful and profoundly merciful. And because somebody has to save Christmas.

THOUGHTS TO CONSIDER:

1. *What is forbearance? How have you seen the Lord's forbearance in the biblical narrative up to this point? What does this mean for you?*

2. *Have you ever actively refused to listen to the Lord? What happened?*

3. *Has being faithful and obedient to the Lord ever cost you anything?*

— twenty-one —

SHADOWS OF PROVIDENCE

*Yet in spite of this, when they are in the land of
their enemies, I will not reject them or abhor them
so as to destroy them completely, breaking my
covenant with them. I am the Lord their God. But
for their sake I will remember the covenant with
their ancestors whom I brought out of Egypt in the
sight of the nations to be their God. I am the Lord.*
Leviticus 26:44-45

Just as Daniel had prayed and God had promised, the
time of exile has come to the end. The Jewish people, who
were taken into captivity by the Babylonians, have been
released by the Persians to go back to their homeland.
Many return to start the process of rebuilding Jerusalem
and the temple, but others remain scattered throughout
the Medo-Persian empire.

Wherever they are dwelling, the Jews now live under
the rule of the Persian government, which is led by a king

named Xerxes. And Xerxes will unwittingly bring Israel to the brink of annihilation.

Strangely enough, at this dark hour in Jewish history, God's name seems to be blatantly hidden from the record. But as we have seen before, when God's name is conspicuously absent, His providence is conspicuously present. That is dramatically true in the story of Esther, in which Scripture carefully avoids mentioning the name of God. Yet every detail in Esther's life is a vivid display of His sovereign hand at work, reshaping world history to ensure the coming of Christmas.

Esther's story begins with a banquet, held by the king to honor...the king. As part of the festivities, he demands that his queen, Vashti, come and parade herself in front of everyone in the capital. She refuses, Xerxes becomes outraged, and he decides to find a new queen.

The king appoints a search committee to scour the countryside and identify the most beautiful young ladies in the land, who will then be subject to a year-long beauty pageant to determine the new queen of Persia. One of those young ladies happens to be a Jewish girl named Esther, an orphan who is being raised by her cousin Mordecai.

At Mordecai's instruction, however, she keeps her Jewish identity a secret.

Esther's beauty and charm cause her to stand out from her peers and to gain "the favor of everyone who saw her" (Esther 2:15), including the king himself. Xerxes places the crown on Esther's head and introduces his subjects to their new queen.

Shortly after his cousin's royal promotion, Mordecai overhears two of Xerxes' officials having a heated political discussion. Their conversation then turns violent—and they begin making plans to assassinate the king! Mordecai scrambles to get word to Esther, so she can warn Xerxes about this treason. The conspirators are caught in time, and the king's life is saved.

In spite of Mordecai's valiant efforts, the king forgets about him when he decides to appoint a new right-hand man. Instead, he reaches into his bank of political leaders and promotes a man named Haman. Haman comes to the job with a bit of an ego problem, and he lets this new role go to his head. He takes great pleasure in parading through the city so that all may bow down to him. But Mordecai won't give him the honor, perhaps because Haman is descended from the Amalekites, the longstanding enemies of Israel. Whatever the reason, this act of defiance wounds Haman's pride so much that he doesn't want to just take revenge on Mordecai, but he wants to wipe out the entire Jewish race!

He appeals to Xerxes' own pride and convinces him to sign off on this insane plan—without the king bothering to ask for details of the edict or the people targeted by it. Haman tells him, "There is a certain people dispersed among the peoples in all the provinces of your kingdom who keep themselves separate. Their customs are different from those of all other people, and they do not obey the king's laws; it is not in the king's best interest to tolerate them" (Esther 3:8).

So the death sentence is written, and Haman rolls some dice, or "lots," to decide which day to carry it out. Fortunately, as Scripture reveals, "the lot is cast into the lap, but its every decision is from the Lord" (Proverbs 16:33).

God is still at work, and His people will not be forgotten. Because somebody has to save Christmas.

THOUGHTS TO CONSIDER:

1. *Have you ever been passed over for a promotion you felt you'd earned or not received the recognition you felt you deserved? How did you deal with that?*

2. *How might God have been at work in the circumstance from the previous question?*

3. *What do you think Proverbs 16:33 means, when it says "every decision is from the Lord"? What are the implications of that statement?*

— *twenty-two* —

SUCH A TIME AS THIS

For if you remain silent at this time, relief and deliverance for the Jews will arise from another place, but you and your father's family will perish. And who knows but that you have come to your royal position for such a time as this?
Esther 4:14

When Mordecai finds out about the grave threat to his people, he tells Esther that she must go before the king and plead their case. Esther initially resists—after all, entering the presence of the king without permission is, in itself, punishable by death. But Mordecai insists. He knows that the people and the promises of God will be preserved somehow, and what if He has chosen Esther for that very purpose? "For if you remain silent at this time, relief and deliverance for the Jews will arise from another place, but you and your father's family will perish. And who knows but that you have come to your royal position for such a time as this?" (Esther 4:14).

Esther is convinced, and she accepts her dangerous mission. She asks for the Jews to gather and fast on her behalf. After that, she says, "I will go to the king, even though it is against the law. And if I perish, I perish" (Esther 4:15).

Three days later, Esther approaches the throne and awaits her fate. Xerxes sees her and—to Esther's great relief—he extends his golden scepter, welcoming her into his presence and sparing her life. Not only that, but he offers to grant any wish that she has, "even up to half the kingdom" (Esther 5:3). She responds by inviting Xerxes— and his evil sidekick Haman—to a banquet.

Haman is, naturally, thrilled by the thought of a private dinner with the king and queen. But his enthusiasm is diminished when he sees Mordecai continuing to defy him. So at the encouragement of his wife and friends, Haman builds a seventy-five foot gallows with which to execute Mordecai. Tomorrow, he plans to visit the king to obtain the execution order.

But that night, Xerxes happens to have trouble sleeping. Since there was no Ambien in those days, he commands his attendants to read aloud the history of his kingdom. When they come to the report of Mordecai's noble act that saved the king's life, Xerxes wants to know how Mordecai was honored for his heroism. It turns out that he wasn't honored at all! Xerxes wants to correct that oversight right away, so he calls for Haman and asks him, "What should be done for the man the king delights to honor?" (Esther 6:6).

Haman, prideful as always, assumes that "the man" Xerxes is referring to is Haman. He suggests that such a prestigious individual should be given the king's robes to wear, a royal horse to ride, and a parade so that everyone can lavish praise upon him. Xerxes thinks that is a great idea, and he tells Haman to go do all of that for *Mordecai.*

Haman fulfills this humiliating request and then, defeated and embittered, he arrives for the banquet with Esther and Xerxes. While they are sharing drinks together, the king once again offers to give his queen whatever it is that her heart desires. She accepts and reveals to the king that there has been a plot against herself and her people, the Jews. Xerxes asks, "Where is he—the man who has dared to do such a thing?" (Esther 7:5).

Esther replies, "An adversary and enemy! This vile Haman!" (Esther 7:6).

The king is furious, and he ends up ordering Haman to be hung on the very gallows he had built to kill Mordecai.

The enemy is dead, yet the threat to the Jewish people is not quite over. Persian custom says that no order of the king can be redacted, and the genocidal edict is still on the books. So Xerxes tells Mordecai that he can write a new law that will allow the Jews to protect themselves from the imminent attack.

When the fateful day finally arrives, the Jewish people rise up and defeat their enemies. They will live on. And so will the promises of God.

Through all of these extraordinary events, God is never even mentioned. Yet we cannot possibly miss the way He has worked to put all of the pieces of the puzzle together. Because somebody has to save Christmas.

THOUGHTS TO CONSIDER:

1. *How does God weave the moral responsibility of man to bring about His promise of Christmas?*

2. *The Lord can leverage something as mundane as insomnia to ensure the promised Seed will arrive on time. What implications or encouragements do you take from that?*

3. *Consider the faith and courage Esther must have had to face the king. Is there something the Lord is calling you to step toward with faith and courage?*

— *twenty-three* —

SILENCE IS BROKEN

You will conceive and give birth to a son, and
you are to call him Jesus. He will be great
and will be called the Son of the Most High.
The Lord God will give him the throne of his
father David, and he will reign over Jacob's
descendants forever; his kingdom will never end.
Luke 1:31-33

Four hundred years go by, with more persecution, more wars, and more unrest in Israel. Yet, as far as we know, the Jews have received no word or revelation from the Lord during that time. No prophets, no miracles, no voice from Heaven. They have the promises recorded in Scripture to cling to, but those promises remain unfulfilled. The Seed of the woman has not yet come to crush the serpent.

But then God quietly begins to raise the curtain for the climactic act of His redemptive drama.

First, He sends His angelic messenger Gabriel to a priest named Zechariah. Like their ancestors Abraham and Sarah, Zechariah and his wife Elizabeth have been unable to have children and are now advanced in age. But Gabriel says that they will indeed have a son, and they are to name him John.

John will have the remarkable mission of preparing God's people for the culmination of His greatest promise. "And he will go on before the Lord, in the spirit and power of Elijah, to turn the hearts of the parents to their children and the disobedient to the wisdom of the righteous—to make ready a people prepared for the Lord" (Luke 1:17).

Six months later, the angel delivers another message to Elizabeth's cousin, Mary. Mary is a young girl who is engaged to a carpenter named Joseph. Gabriel tells Mary that she, too, is about to have a son. And not just any son—but the Son whom Israel has been anticipating for generations, the Son of God and the Son of David who will rule and reign forever.

Mary is surprised, to say the least. "Then Mary said to the angel, 'How can this be, since I do not know a man?'" (Luke 1:34 NKJV).

The reply from Gabriel is even more amazing. He informs Mary that the Holy Spirit will come upon her, and that her baby will be conceived supernaturally. Just as God had once revealed to the prophet Isaiah, "the virgin will conceive and give birth to a son, and will call him Immanuel" (Isaiah 7:14b).

As one might expect, Mary's fiancé is also taken aback by her pregnancy. He assumes the worst, but since he is a kind man, he intends to break off the engagement as discreetly as possible. Then he gets his own divine instruction. "But after he had considered this, an angel of the Lord appeared to him in a dream and said, 'Joseph son of David, do not be afraid to take Mary home as your wife, because what is conceived in her is from the Holy Spirit. She will give birth to a son, and you are to give him the name Jesus, because he will save his people from their sins'" (Matthew 1:20-21).

The silence has been broken. The prophecies are coming true. And the wait is almost over. Because somebody has to save Christmas.

THOUGHTS TO CONSIDER:

1. *Why is it significant that Jesus would be born from a virgin?*

2. *How does our sin nature manifest itself in everyday life?*

3. *What is something you've had to wait expectantly for? Do you find it difficult to trust God in times of waiting? Why or why not?*

— *twenty-four* —

LITTLE TOWN WITH A BIG PURPOSE

But you, Bethlehem Ephrathah, though you are small among the clans of Judah, out of you will come for me one who will be ruler over Israel, whose origins are from of old, from ancient times.
Micah 5:2

The pieces are finally in place for Christmas to arrive. A virgin is pregnant, and she is almost ready to give birth to the most significant baby ever born. There's just one problem: God had declared that the anticipated Redeemer would be born in Bethlehem, but Joseph and Mary are eighty miles away in Nazareth.

This is no trivial matter. If any of God's prophecies do not come to pass, then all hope in His promises will be lost. Christmas must take place in Bethlehem, so if Joseph and Mary don't travel there soon, there can be no Christmas.

Entering the scene to save the day is a most unexpected—and unwitting—hero: Caesar Augustus, the ruler of the Roman Empire, of which the Jewish people are now a part. "In those days Caesar Augustus issued a decree that a census should be taken of the entire Roman world" (Luke 2:1).

In order to fulfill the requirements of this census, Roman subjects would all need to return to their ancestral homes to register their families. Even though his fiancée is on the verge of having a baby, Joseph obeys the order. "So Joseph also went up from the town of Nazareth in Galilee to Judea, to Bethlehem the town of David, because he belonged to the house and line of David. He went there to register with Mary, who was pledged to be married to him and was expecting a child" (Luke 2:4).

Joseph and Mary begin their journey to Bethlehem, obeying a government edict but ultimately fulfilling the Word of God. Now the stage is set for the moment to arrive that Israel—and the entirety of creation—has been waiting for ever since Adam and Eve ate the forbidden fruit.

As the hymn says about that little town of Bethlehem, "The hopes and fears of all the years are met in thee tonight." History has yearned for this day, knowing that somebody has to save Christmas.

THOUGHTS TO CONSIDER

1. *How does obedience to authority play a significant role in saving Christmas? Do you find obedience to authority to be a struggle? Why or why not?*

2. *What do you think the Lord may be teaching us in this account regarding the importance of submitting to those over us, even when it is difficult to do so?*

3. *What specific hopes and fears do you have that you can trust Jesus to fulfill? What would it look like to trust Him with those?*

— *twenty-five* —

CHRISTMAS HAS COME

*For my eyes have seen your salvation, which
you have prepared in the sight of all nations:
a light for revelation to the Gentiles, and the
glory of your people Israel.*
Luke 2:30-32

One might expect the pivotal moment in history to be surrounded by the grandest of fanfare—fireworks blasting, trumpets sounding, triumphant voices shouting. But when the promised Savior is born, He ends up being placed in a feeding trough because there isn't even a room available for Joseph and Mary (Luke 2:6-7). The humble setting belies the majesty of this moment: *The promised Seed has arrived.*

Nearby, there are shepherds caring for their flocks in, perhaps, the same fields where young David was working when he received his royal calling so many years before. Their night is interrupted by a divine messenger, sent to tell them that the eternal King has finally come. "But the angel said to them, 'Do not be afraid. I bring you good news that will cause great joy for all the people. Today in the town of David a Savior has been born to you; he is the Messiah, the Lord'" (Luke 2:10-11).

The centuries of waiting are over. The Rescuer who the world has so desperately needed is here. God has shaped history to make sure that Christmas would come right on time. No detail has escaped His attention, and nothing could knock His plans off course.

God used kings to prepare the way for the King of kings. He used princes to pave a path for the Prince of Peace. He used shepherds to herald the coming of the Good Shepherd. He used the sons of men to give us the Son of Man. He used slaves to bring the One who would set the captives free. He used sinners to ensure the arrival of the One who would become sin for them.

He used the murder of a brother, the faithlessness of a father, the deceptiveness of a mother and son, the deceit of an uncle, and the competition between sisters to bring about His chosen people. To protect that people, and to preserve the Seed He promised, He used a brother's betrayal, a butler's forgetfulness, a pharaoh's dream, a princess's bath, a ruler's insomnia.

He spoke through a burning bush. He parted waters. He dropped bread from heaven. He destroyed enemies. He used famines and favoritism, arks and adultery, plagues and pride.

He used defiant midwives, a daring prostitute, a persistent daughter-in-law, a courageous queen, and a humble virgin. He used righteous kings and wicked kings, old men and young men, heroes and villains, the faithful and the faithless. God took the good, bad, and ugly of mankind and used them to bring the story of redemption to its glorious fulfillment. The powers of sin, death, and hell could not stop this baby from being born in Bethlehem. All of the efforts of the evil one to prevent that birth were futile. And now the Seed of the woman has come to crush him.

Because somebody had to save Christmas.

THOUGHTS TO CONSIDER:

1. *Have you ever considered that you are part of the present, ongoing story of redemption to usher in Jesus' second coming? What are the implications of this for your life?*

2. *Do you ever struggle to see yourself as significant? As you've read through this book, what stands out to you about people whom God chose to use? How might He use your faithful obedience to advance His kingdom?*

3. *How has your perspective of Christmas changed after reading this book?*

CONCLUSION

One of the many reasons that we believe the Scriptures are true is this amazing story of how God saved Christmas. Consider the fact that the narratives we have surveyed in this book were penned by dozens of writers who lived in different parts of the Middle East and were often separated by hundreds of years. Yet together they perfectly weaved the tapestry of salvation. It is well beyond the scope of any human understanding.

As we have traced the story of Christmas through the pages of Scripture, we hope that it has caused you to stand in awe of the all-knowing, all-powerful God who brought all of this to pass. And whether these stories have been familiar to you, or whether they are all brand new, we pray that the words of this book might encourage you to go back to the source and read the full story in the Bible.

You'll discover that the story doesn't stop at Christmas. That baby in the manger grew up to live a sinless life, fulfilling every aspect of God's law perfectly. He died on a cross to take the punishment for the sins of the world, and then He was raised to life again three days later, so that we could live together with Him forever.

The angels declared to those shepherds in Bethlehem that a *Savior* had been born. What does a Savior do? He *saves*. And we need saving. We are in such dire straits that we could do nothing to save ourselves. So when Jesus saves us, it is not accomplished through a mixture of our efforts and His. It's all Him. If we try to contribute to our own salvation through good works, then Christ becomes a helper, not a Savior. We can never be good enough to save ourselves. Does that mean we shouldn't even try? By no means. Doing good flows out of our love for what Christ has done for us, not as an effort to earn His love. Good deeds and righteous living are a response to Jesus' love, never a means to earn or repay it. If we miss that point, even though we say we believe in Jesus, we miss the whole point of Christianity. This is how you can tell counterfeit Christianity from the real thing: *Authentic Christianity trusts in the* finished *work of Christ while counterfeit Christianity trusts in* finishing *the work of Christ.*

Christmas isn't about a holiday or a time of year. It's about a Person. It's about the One whom God promised He would send to reverse the curse of sin and to reconcile sinful people with their Creator. It's about the One who lived the life we could never live and died the death we deserved to die.

And Christmas is about gifts, right? Well, there is no greater gift than the gift of salvation.

"For the wages of sin is death, but the gift of God is eternal life in Christ Jesus our Lord" (Romans 6:23). "For it is by grace you have been saved, through faith—and this is not from yourselves, it is the gift of God—not by works, so that no one can boast" (Ephesians 2:8-9).

And a gift is, by its very essence, freely given. It is not something earned, deserved, or repaid. Scripture makes it abundantly clear that our salvation is given out of God's love and mercy, and that we can take zero credit for it.

"He saved us, not because of righteous things we had done, but because of his mercy" (Titus 3:5a). "Now to the one who works, wages are not credited as a gift but as an obligation. However, to the one who does not work but trusts God who justifies the ungodly, their faith is credited as righteousness" (Romans 4:4-5).

If you haven't already received this free gift of salvation, what better time is there than right now? You only need to acknowledge your sin before a holy God and call upon Him to save you through Jesus Christ, and then you will immediately be rescued from the power of darkness and placed into the Kingdom of God's dear Son (Colossians 1:13). Get the matter settled today, and this will be the best Christmas you have ever had.

Now you know how God used many people to save Christmas—so that Christmas could save many people.

Are you one of them?